# 30 Gospel Arrangements for Old Time Banjo

Matthew Allen

# CONTENTS

# Amazing Grace (Clawhammer)

(Banjo)

gDGBD Tuning

# Amazing Grace (2FTL)

(Banjo)

gDGBD Tuning

# Amazing Grace (2FIL)

(Banjo)

gDGBD Tuning

# Are You Washed In The Blood (Clawhammer)

(Banjo)

gDGBD Tuning

# Are You Washed In The Blood (2FTL)

### (Banjo)

**gDGBD Tuning**

# Are You Washed In The Blood (2FIL)

(Banjo)

gDGBD Tuning

# Glory To His Name (Clawhammer)

(Banjo)

gDGBD Tuning

# Glory To His Name (2FTL)

(Banjo)

gDGBD Tuning

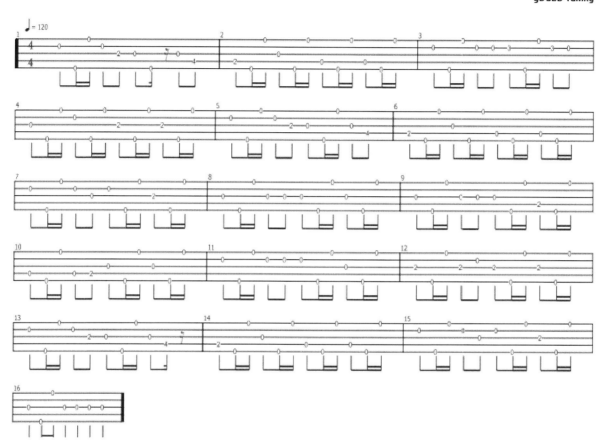

# Glory To His Name (2FIL)

## (Banjo)

**gDGBD Tuning**

# Leaning On The Everlasting Arms (Clawhammer)

(Banjo)

gDGBD Tuning

# Leaning On The Everlasting Arms (2FTL)

## (Banjo)

gDGBD Tuning

# Leaning On The Everlasting Arms (2FIL)

### (Banjo)

gDGBD Tuning

# Nothing But The Blood (Clawhammer)

(Nothing But The Blood)

gDGBD Tuning

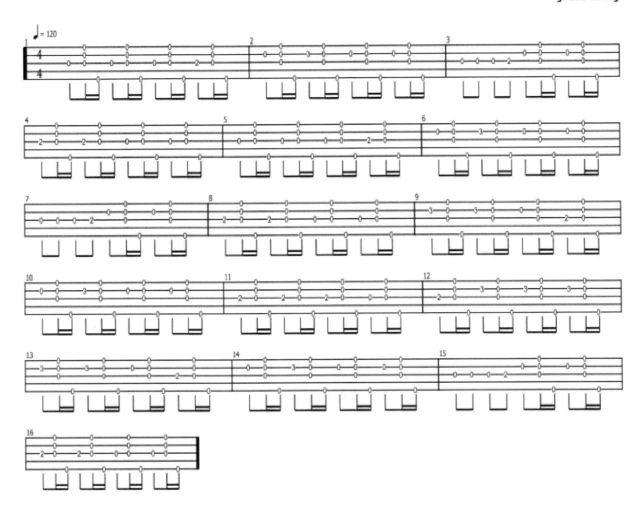

# Nothing But The Blood (2FTL)

(Nothing But The Blood)

gDGBD Tuning

# Nothing But The Blood (2FIL)

(Nothing But The Blood)

gDGBD Tuning

# Power In The Blood (Clawhammer)

(Banjo)

gDGBD Tuning

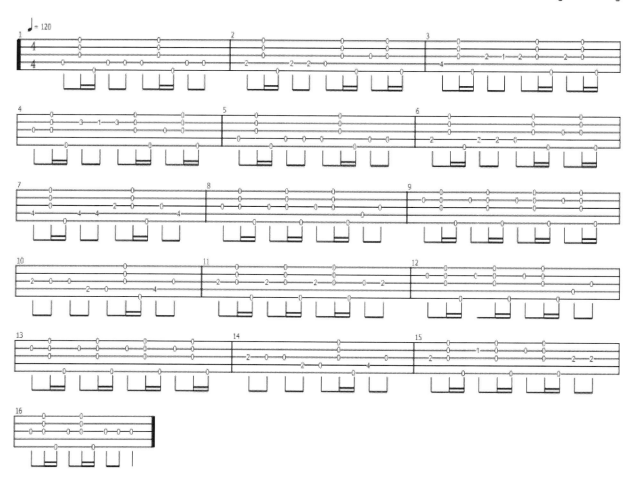

# Power In The Blood (2FTL)

(Banjo)

gDGBD Tuning

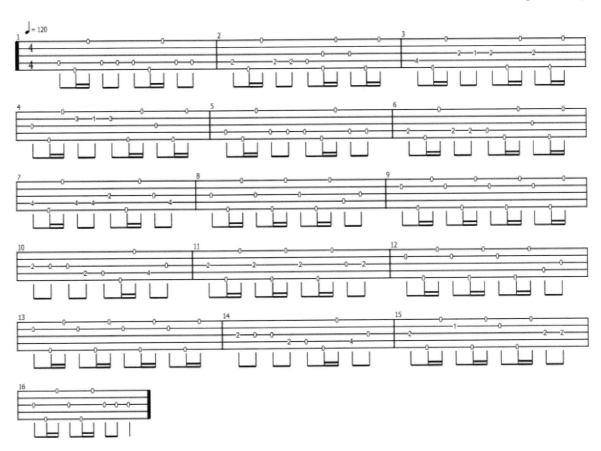

# Power In The Blood (2FIL)

(Banjo)

**gDGBD Tuning**

# Stand Up, Stand Up For Jesus

(Banjo)

gDGBD Tuning

# Stand Up, Stand Up For Jesus (2FTL)

### (Banjo)

gDGBD Tuning

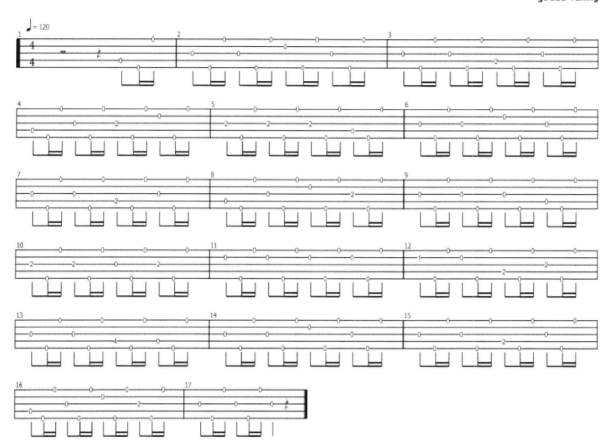

# Stand Up, Stand Up For Jesus (2FIL)

(Banjo)

gDGBD Tuning

# Sweet By And By (Clawhammer)

(Banjo)

gDGBD Tuning

# Sweet By And By (2FTL)

(Banjo)

gDGBD Tuning

# Sweet By And By (2FIL)

(Banjo)

**gDGBD Tuning**

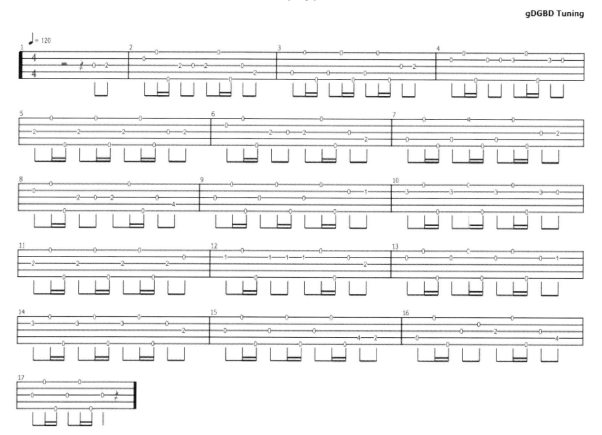

# What A Friend We Have In Jesus

(Banjo)

gDGBD Tuning

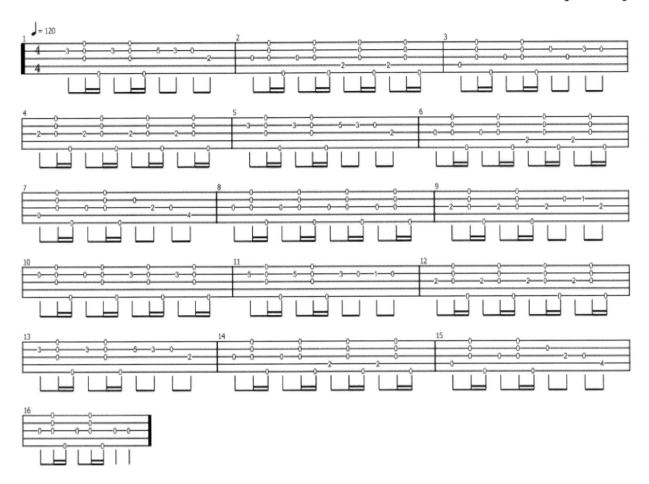

# What A Friend We Have In Jesus (2FTL)

(Banjo)

gDGBD Tuning

# What A Friend We Have In Jesus (2FIL)

(Banjo)

gDGBD Tuning

# When The Roll Is Called Up Yonder (Clawhammer)

(Banjo)

gDGBD Tuning

# When The Roll Is Called Up Yonder (2FTL)

(Banjo)

**gDGBD Tuning**

# When The Roll Is Called Up Yonder (2FIL)
(Banjo)

gDGBD Tuning

Printed in Great Britain
by Amazon